Say Anything

poems prose poems

Lee Rossi

Plain View Press, LLC
1101 W 34th Street, STE 404

www.plainviewpress.com
Austin, TX 78705

Copyright © 2024 Lee Rossi. All rights reserved under International and Pan-American Copyright Conventions. No part of this book may be reproduced or distributed in any form or by any means, or stored in a data base or retrieval system, without written permission from the author. All rights, including electronic, are reserved by the author and publisher.

ISBN: 978-1-63210-099-3
ebook ISBN: 978-1-63210-100-6
Library of Congress Control Number: 2023940555

Cover art by Loretta Young-Gautier
Cover design by Pam Knight

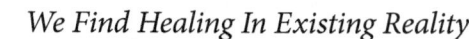

We Find Healing In Existing Reality

Plain View Press is a 45-year-old issue-based literary publishing house. Our books result from artistic collaboration between writers, artists, and editors. Over the years we have become a far-flung community of humane and highly creative activists whose energies bring humanitarian enlightenment and hope to individuals and communities grappling with the major issues of our time—peace, justice, the environment, education and gender.

Say Anything

poems prose poems

Lee Rossi

Also by Lee Rossi

Darwin's Garden (Moon Tide Press, 2019)
Wheelchair Samurai (Plainview Press, 2011)
Ghost Diary (Terrapin Press, 2003)
Beyond Rescue (Bombshelter Press, 1992)

for Elisabeth, Leo & Evelyn—
may all families be so loving

Contents

Introduction—A Deep Dive		9
Primo		**11**
microcosmology		13
Surveillance		**15**
Consider This		17
Cricket		18
Say Anything		19
Antinomies		21
Instructions to My Teenage Self		22
Sebastian to His Wounds		23
The Retired Epistemologist		24
Apply Topically		25
The Angel Angle		26
Speech Axe		27
Cracks and Leaks		**29**
Rules of Thumb		31
Gone Wild		32
Spirit Train		33
Scenes From the Other Life		34
No! Not That!		35
Close Encounters of Another Kind		36
The International House of Insomnia		37
Zen—The Video Game		39
"I Hate This Tree"		**41**
Portrait of the Artist As a Young Fashionista		43
Hymn to Ninkasi		45
Horizon and Walls		46
The Case of the Missing Chicken Pot Pie		48

Sacrifice Fly	49
Rats and Squirrels	51
Young Americans for Freedom	52
Magnolia	54
Top of the Chain	56
For I Will Consider My Dog Riley	58
Butterfly	60
Clipped	62
Culture Vultures	**65**
Wirtschaftswunderkind	67
Many Are Called	69
Match	71
No Sweat (the Step Reebok Poem)	73
Kaffee mit Schlag	74
Peeling the Onion	76
Belles de Jour	78
Boardom	80
Forgetfulness	82
Not Brave, Not Free	83
Passing an Evening, Not Quite Drunk	84
Journée Internationale de la Bisexualité	86
Ultimo	**89**
underwater	91
About the Author	93
Acknowledgments	95

Introduction—A Deep Dive

This is my fifth book of poetry. I can't seem to break the habit. As soon as I finish one book, I start thinking about the next. Thinking may be too strong a word. What happens is I start looking at new poems and poems that didn't make it into the last book, arranging and re-arranging them to see if and how they fit with one another.

One of my teachers, Peter Levitt, used to say that the imagination is whole. I'm not sure what he meant by that. Personally, I suspect that my personality is like those pieces of colored glass that you find in a kaleidoscope. Looked at one way, they might be red and jagged. Looked at another way, they're a jumble of green. But that's MY personality, not THE imagination, which apparently I cannot claim for myself, but which belongs to us all, the world ocean in which we all swim, in which we feed and communicate.

I've had many teachers. I love them all (even the ones I didn't like). All of them have helped me overcome my fear of drowning. In fact, I was so afraid of drowning I might never have ventured a swim. It takes time and practice to trust oneself in such a large body of water. Every poem is a new experience of that ocean, a record of that experience.

The poems in this new book are different, I think, than those in the last. My last book was an attempt to catch up with my younger contemporaries, poets whose engagement with political and social issues outstripped mine. As I started looking at newer poems, I realized that the way I wanted to say things was changing. I found myself in the grip of unresolvable contradictions, whose most frequent mode of expression was oxymoron and paradox. My subject was shifting, from my exterior, historical, biographical reality, to an inner psychological reality, from a world of fact and idea, to a world of nuance and shadow.

Maybe that's enough to say about this book. Maybe it's too much. I hope you enjoy these poems as much as I enjoyed the process of discovery.

Lee Rossi
12/31/2022

Primo

microcosmology

Everything fits into everything else.
We know that who come bursting
from our mothers in a gush of being,
our children already nestled in sacs
tucked safely inside. Infinite regression
sends us back into the womb
after womb from which we grew.
There was a soup, we're told,
where the first living creatures
were brewed, not something you'd
eat, but eat it they apparently did
until there was nothing left but waste
oxygen and each other.
How long did they take to find
a taste for those other squirming
thinglets—eat it or fuck it,
and in which order, the rush
to colonize never stopped.
Except in imagination,
we can't stuff ourselves
back into that ever-expanding bottle,
which itself was once just something
infinitely dense, unimaginably hot,
and before that not even not.

Surveillance

"If a tree falls in the forest and no one hears it . . . "

—George Berkeley

Consider This

I like poets who think in their poems.
I myself am incapable of thought.
Every time I try I end up

in contradiction or tautology.
Thinking is one of those expensive
cul-de-sacs with no way in

and no way out. The folks who live
there are happy with their neighbors,
content with their four-thousand

square feet of rapture, their patios,
bar-b-ques, and infinity pools.
No friend visits but neither do strangers

or the homeless. Sipping mai-tais
they shade their eyes from the sky-
borne glare, waving wistfully

as helicopters and commercial jets
thunder by. Meanwhile I find myself
wandering along some unfamiliar street

stunned by the roar of traffic, another
passer-by stranded in the present.

Cricket

If I use the word God in a poem,
does it mean I believe in God—
or that I don't? Once upon a time

God was the water we swam in.
Do fish thank the water for letting them swim?
When I was 17, I wrote my first poem,

but stopped writing six months later.
I didn't want to be a confessional poet
with nothing to confess.

Guilt, I had plenty of that,
the way that tall grass has chiggers.
My conscience sang like a field

of crickets. It was only the sun,
you might say, warming them
like pots on a stove, as natural

as banana skins going black,
but I wanted to believe that Someone
was watching my every move,

keeping track in some record book.
Don't you see? Without some Gentle Jailer surveilling
everything, my kind of life, small

as a chigger or a cricket,
would go unremarked. And now, at 76,
I don't know what to believe.

I watch the grasses dry and whiten,
the stream trickle to a standstill,
and still I sing that one field,

the long grasses,
the bright and withering sun.

Say Anything

At first I couldn't say anything.
I was a bobbin wound with silk

beginning its long migration
through skirt or inseam, hemming

and hawing. I was afraid of truth
and so was given many truths,

all of them huddled
on the leeward side of the cliff.

I didn't speak to the cliff,
and it did not speak to me.

I spoke instead to my mother,
her roots diving into the restless soil

like genies who forget their powers,
the power to reverse time,

the power to make the dead see
who they really are,

and thus be revived.
My mother spoke quietly

shaping the wind into syllables,
a language I would never learn to speak.

Don't get me wrong.
I did learn to speak.

There was fire, and buildings
tumbled to the ground.

I searched and found
plastic forks, plastic dolls, tricycles.

I wore them around my neck—
amulets against the future,

or the past. But now I've given up my search.
(You knew that.)

I have found as much of the truth as I can carry,
and even so, it's too much,

this load of wood, this raven feather,
each step pushing me deeper into the ground.

Antinomies

I was wrong, I tell myself,
echoing my mother's words—
what she'd say to my father in bed,

both of them fast asleep,
while their spirits circled the trembling house,
my spirit, a silvery char, chasing them

back to their pen, the pen I'd built
for them
            spectators—there were none—
haunted the upper branches, shivering

on their perches—the sudden flare
of wing, blood brightness rushing
to their eyes—such strange visions

interrupting our journey into dawn
the ground fog of night slowly dissipating—
how else explain my restlessness

my gift for yap and bark, except
those nights, leaf-littered
every dark thing moon-illumined

Instructions to My Teenage Self

the next time you go for a walk in the world
remember the stories you heard as a child

a girl goes to visit her grandmother
two kids get lost in the woods—

those stories—
remember, the woods are not just woods but the whole world

and everyone you meet there
is either a wolf or a witch

they may not look like a wolf, or a witch
they may look like your grandmother, some kindly old lady or

like some cool dude who knows his way around
they may even look like you

but don't forget the stories
all they want is to eat you

even your parents
by the time you get home

if you get home
you won't recognize them, or rather

you'll recognize them for the first time
the wolf and the witch you've been living with all along

by now, you're part wolf, part witch yourself
how do I know? who am I?

I'm a bird, a bug, the woods, the wind
I'm that other part of you

the part that's left
after all else has been eaten

Sebastian to His Wounds

I love you, little mouths,
portals through which my life passes—
tell them who I am.

Tell the feathered arrows that though they fly
straighter than birds they cannot find
what remains invisible, undying.

Tell the bows that they can bend
like ash trees in a storm or like a crowd
beneath the orator's words,

yet what remains invisible does not bend.
And tell the strings that sing like lyres
when the notched and feathered arrows fly

like startled flocks at the captain's cry,
that the song of the invisible flies
where they cannot.

Tell the archers, guards and friends,
to find themselves in what pours
joyously from your lips.

And tell my friend and benefactor,
the Emperor who holds us all
in his unforgiving hands,

that when we meet on the final day,
invisible no longer,
you will whisper his name and kiss.

The Retired Epistemologist

lives next door to the Answer Man
across the street from Mrs. Take It On Faith,

having emptied his bath of corrosive skepticism
and watched it whirlpool down the drain.

He can make anything work now—
cold fusion, intelligent design . . .

God is his favorite tool,
applied like duct tape to any leaky idea.

He's got rust in his pipes
and refuses to sing in the choir.

None of his words mean anything
to the world as will and idea.

Sex is a pastime for indigents
and no longer any of his business.

He's forgotten how he survived childhood,
crossing all those Rubicons without the help of allegory.

He has arrived at the confluence
of Knowing and Not Caring,

both streams overflowing their banks,
flood water in the stadium

up to the luxury boxes. Now he will have
to move further inland

even if the storms there are stronger
than the cogito.

He picks up some coins
and walks into the rain.

Apply Topically

The poem of the moment aspires
to the coherence of the bipolar mind.

Some say that ethics is a matter of power:
might makes rightists.

Aprés le déluge Hawaii will be a reef
for tourists without a place to land.

Aquinas hears Kant's confession
before treating him to Kaffee mit Schlag.

The Angelic Doctor blesses the paraplegic
selling pencils outside the Konditorei

then hands him a buck. Responsibility
and guilt are the Siamese twins

of civilized life. Anyone who claims
that men in tribes are more moral

than men in cities hasn't spent enough
time in either place. Oder?

What is that smell, the bodies of our
enemies, manuring our fields,

or the bodies of our children,
thrown recklessly to our ideals?

Get the hell out of my circle,
the demon told Dante, demanding publication

rights to his own story. Imagination,
just another slaughtered innocent.

The Angel Angle

> *Why aren't we more terrified of sleep,*
> *of consciousness extinguished and no*
> *guarantee of return?*
> —Dean Young

You'd think that after all these years
of dropping dead every night and every morning
rolling back the stone, of rising from my vampire's crypt,
a forest of tooth picks sprouting from my chest,
I'd have some faith, some trust that just like
the sun coming up in the east I'd lift
from my cluttered bed, my rumpled, sweat-
soaked sheets and pillow. Don't I believe
in physics? What about bio-chemistry? But no.
After five hundred lives, the memory
of so many deaths darkens everything.
Every day the ceiling gets lower,
clouds rumbling with comets and jets.
And what do they tell you for comfort?
Think about the after-life, they say.
But that's all I think about. Or
Forget about it, they say, it's a long way off.
But how can I forget, when even in sleep
I have to listen to that raving madman
(myself!) shouting out the mystery of birth,
my constant mistakes. How many dark alleys
have you wandered in your dreams, how many
monsters met and been devoured by?
I'm telling you, if I could say goodbye to it all,
become an angel, one of those who never said no
to anyone but himself, one of the luminous
singing host who never traveled in darkness,
I'd take up my wings and sweep
the closets and corners of my past
with a mighty shiver and flap, blowing
it all away as I rose into a glory like the sun.

Speech Axe

If I should axe the symbol of forests, who would hear me? The drones, radiating their own unique sound signature? The earthworms tunneling beneath the hardscape?

Men with hoses and ladders are approaching the scene of the devastation, volunteers are here to pick up the pieces.

My name is not Joe. Although that's what my dad always called me. Joe, or Guisepp'. He also called me Brother.

A tree grows in Brooklyn / Palo Alto / Omaha, waiting to be sent back where it came from.

I'll trade you two Pikachu for one Sonic the Hedgehog.

Can you identify the organ of generation? In my baby pictures a hole punch has removed the organ of generation. This is more than symbolic.

This is a matter of principle: scribo ergo sum.

The glare off concrete relays an invitation to spring, illuminating the stormy underside of clouds, puffs of white cotton swabbing the afternoon's fevered dishpan.

The driver of the Camaro didn't see the protesters, he saw bales of hay with bullseye targets affixed, he saw microscope slides plated with virus, he saw red, white and black.

The boy, who was almost a god, was too beautiful by even divine standards, and so had to die. Die but die painfully, torn by beauty and its loss.

"We'll miss him, of course. (Of course he was a preening, self-important prick.) But maybe it's better this way."

He would've made a good god, not a nice god perhaps, but someone to envy and despise.

But then there was no place to put him. The yard was full, the hothouse too. And you know what happens when you try to bring something that big into the (contemporary suburban home)!

The canopy alone would consume all the breathable air in even the largest living room (with certain possible exceptions in Bel Air and Malibu). And those roots!

Delving the yard like oars in a wine-dark sea. What a monument! What a monstrosity!

But where could you go in such a floundering wreck, that overloaded ferry, chockablock with tourists and camper vans and doubles? The first big blowhard and the thing'd capsize.

And yet every day we fare forth from the same port, the same rust bucket, never knowing for sure when we'll arrive.

Cracks and Leaks

"If you meet the Buddha on the road, kill him."

—Zen Master Linji

Rules of Thumb

That the reason for any action is buried beneath two or three coats of paint. That a foundation lives longer than any other part of the house but will crack and decay, just like a motor mount or the motor in your chest. When caulk dries, a tear streaks a child's dirty face, the lobes of the bishop's miter swell. Think of all the things that dry and crack—paint, caulk, even glass sags given enough time. When you look outside, there is light bringing grass and neighbors. This means they exist even if you never speak to them, breathing your air before it gets to you. Think of all the shelters you've found—a snow fort, a cave, a hole in a road cut, a pair of hands. When a young man turns his back to the sun, this means that the grove has stripped herself for winter. This means yes, that a harsh light rakes the ground and a widow's mottled hands. People move through the house brushing teeth, cooking Spam, arguing and making love, like thoughts in the dream space of the skull. That a house turns many faces to the world. Grim to strangers, it smiles on friends, shielding you from other people's pain. Now go inside and rest.

Gone Wild

    Whenever a boy would disappear, they'd say he'd gone wild, confident he'd come back as a fox or a coyote. Never a gopher or a mole. If they lost a chicken, they'd say it was Cousin Tom or Billy the barber's kid done it. That's why they never shot 'em, just shot at 'em, over their heads or into the woods. It was like they were sayin', we know you're out there and you're not coming back. We know you still need us. But don't need us too much. The girls, of course, never came back, not even as gophers or moles. Or if they did, it was as something in the fox's mouth, something still alive but just barely.

Spirit Train

In the morning I went to the station. It was an old building, surrounded by other old buildings, a bank, a church, and museums for everything the army had stolen in the last war. The station was almost empty, so I asked the Station Master's daughter, "How do I get from Prague to Chicago?" And she said, "You'll have to do what people did back in the War. You'll have to take the Spirit Train." "I don't want to die," I told her. "You don't have to," she said, "but you'll have to change many times." That sounded bad enough, but I wanted to get home. So I found a bench in the Great Hall and waited. I guess I fell asleep, because the next thing I knew someone was shaking my shoulder. "It's after midnight, time to go," she said, the same girl but older. I found the train, and soon we were moving through the countryside. At first, I was a dog, a water spaniel, and then a giant boar. When we got to the coast, I changed into a tuna, then a shad, a mackerel, a school of mackerel. We were moving very fast, and I couldn't keep track of all the changes. Soon we arrived at another coast where I became a turkey, then a vole, a freshwater trout, a mole, a catfish, a mule deer, and then finally as we pulled into Chicago, a man. I should be glad, I suppose, that I didn't spend much time as an insect. My parents were waiting there in Chicago. (How did they know to meet me?) With a girl, who looked familiar, but whose name escaped me. All of them hugged me, and I guess I hugged them back. I didn't know what to say. I didn't know how to act. And it's been that way ever since.

Scenes From the Other Life

One time you're walking alone in a long hall, a hall that is not unfamiliar—you've walked so many halls in your life—but which you don't recognize. The walls are gray and every so often there's a door, a dark gray metal door with a number. The sheet in your hand has a number, the number of the room you're looking for, but the sheet is wet, wet or drying, and the number is smeared, almost legible. You hope you're close. You read the number on the nearest door. You try the door. There are people inside, but are they the right people?

Another time you're walking along a street, a narrow winding street in a foreign city. The houses, which are old, three or four stories tall, lean into the street above your head. You've been here before—if not this exact street, then some other that is nearby. You've forgotten what you're looking for. A shop, a bar, a person maybe? There's no one else on the street. Where are the people you came with? Did they leave you? Did you leave them? You notice that there are no shops on the street, no windows at street level.

Another time, you're in a large industrial building. The space is dark, but you can feel it extending high into the air. There's someone with you. You don't know her name, but you want to be alone with her. You want to find a room somewhere where you can be alone with her. You walk deeper into the building, up a set of stairs, along a catwalk, another set of stairs. You find a corridor that curves to the left. Maybe you'll find a room, a janitor's closet, if you keep walking. You try a door, a locked door. You throw yourself against it. You try another door, which opens. There's nothing to see, only gray walls and a concrete floor. You turn to your companion, but she's gone.

Another time, you're in a room rehearsing a play. You're puzzled. You have a bad memory, but they've given you the biggest part in the play. Everybody's looking to you to remember your part. You look at someone. She looks familiar, someone you used to live with maybe, someone who is no longer alive. She takes your hand and leads you outside, into the cool evening air. She puts her arm around your shoulder. You put your arm around her waist, and begin to cry.

No! Not That!

The doctor says to take off my clothes. My clothes don't come off in front of anyone, not even my wife. They're very particular. They'd be embarrassed for me. And I appreciate their discretion. The doctor wants to look for things on my skin that might be cancer. I might bare my skin to the sun, but not to the doctor. Of course I don't bare my skin to the sun anymore. I hide inside my clothes. It's better that way for everyone. I'm a tree shrouded in fog. I'm a winter storm that closes the airport, the view from the window like static on your high-definition TV. I'm the rock slide blocking the coast highway. The doctor tells me not to be embarrassed, she does this twenty-four times a day, every 20 minutes for eight hours a day. This does not help, even after I've removed my shirt and returned it to the snow melt that used to be a snow man, even after I've lowered my easy-on, easy-off gym pants, the ones with the swoosh. Her hands, the only part of her that I can see besides her face, are purple. Don't touch that, I want to say, and she touches it, looking right, looking left, and then she's on to the rear. I want to scream, but I don't. I'll be coming back in 3 to 6 months. That's what they do to people who've had skin cancer, but she won't be here. She's got lots of good colleagues and in the meantime she'll be adding another child to her collection. She's got one, a 3-year-old, already. I try not to think about another visit. I try not to think about cancer. I am a one-man golf cart delivering my rider to the dinner table three times a day.

Close Encounters of Another Kind

F. now realizes that she should have paid closer attention in her exo-biology class. At the time she didn't care that this particular species, whom she always thought of as "the Blob" could fashion its pseudopodia into any form of appendage—head, or arms and legs, her favorites being dorsal fins and the ridge of plates favored by Stegosaurus—all quite convincing. No wonder they spread so quickly through the known planets, these deft infiltrators, able to mimic the exact outlines of any apex predator.

What she was looking at was a fairly brawny male of her own species, totally naked and sporting a giant penis, the size of a large flash light. The fact that they were both floating in the zero gravity of her space ship made the encounter almost laughable. Would her laughter have become alarm if she'd remembered the creature's ability to simulate not just the form but the chemistry, in this instance the sexual chemistry, of target species, chemistry which at the moment was causing her to focus almost exclusively on the large red pseudo-glans aimed at her oral cavity.

After that particular docking maneuver, performed with more than the usual enthusiasm, a certain recklessness even, they tried others, all of them fairly pleasant—at least in her current state of chemically induced euphoria. Give him credit, she thought, he puts the X in extra-terrestrial.

How she escaped the creature's ever-changing clutches, she couldn't remember. Maybe he simply left. They do that. Maybe she blasted him into his constituent molecules—she had done that, more than once—which in any case were now being filtered from her air and water supply. All she knew was that one morning she awoke to find her bed filled with a clutch of small needy creatures, which looked vaguely like herself, only blobular. Oh well, she had always wanted to be a mother. No reason to think her situation, floating out there all alone, would be any different if the Blob had been human. Sometimes fake is just as good as the real thing.

The International House of Insomnia

It was the last can of paper straws in the Western United States, and William the Conquered had already used and discarded half of them, a process that had taken barely a month of malts, shakes and Diet Cokes not to mention smoothies, slushies and homemade slurpies. When it became clear that not even the internet was going to save him—that the whole rest of the world, India included, had switched to those perfectly extruded green and red plastic tubes they gave away at Macdonald's and 7-Eleven, he began rinsing and re-using them. Rinsing didn't completely eliminate the taste of his previous meal—cherry and chocolate left the most residue or at least the most taste—but it did help. It meant that the next liquid had to be thicker and stronger tasting than the last, and that only hastened the straw's demise.

But for the moment he could only eat or drink with a straw, and for whatever reason, it had to be a paper straw, the kind with the thin helical join (often colored) starting at one end and spiraling to the other, thereby providing strength and visual interest.

That was one thing that bothered him about contemporary straws—despite their intense neon colors, they were all the same, the same green or red or sparkle pattern, the same smooth inviolable texture—a rifle barrel without the rifling.

He noted that there was probably something wrong with him, in addition to all the conditions known to his doctor and psychiatrist, something that paper straws could only salve but not cure. But he was running out of straws, and very soon he was going to have a very big problem. Of course, he realized that people in Chekhov didn't have these problems. He was always reading Chekhov's stories and always reading himself into Chekhov's characters. It was easier than being himself. But their problems didn't encompass the disappearance of a basic tool of domestic life, or if they did, they did so in a way which escaped his limited understanding of nineteenth-century Russian life and technology.

Besides, he'd never met a Chekhov character who suffered from his particular dental pathology. His teeth had the disturbing habit of cracking and splitting whenever he bit down on something harder than a jelly bean. Maybe it came from all those years cracking unpopped kernels of popcorn. Now whenever he chewed burnt toast a sliver of enamel would calve from his tooth like an Antarctic iceberg. But maybe that was only his "presenting symptom." Maybe there was more to his condition than he suspected.

Zen—The Video Game

Level 1 begins at a mountain monastery overlooking the Napa Valley in northern California. You are working in the organic garden with a group of monks. Your job is to loosen the soil with a shovel. You've never worked with your hands, so despite the cold, you are soon sweating. Suddenly you are attacked by a pack of demons in the shape of wolves. You have barely a second to raise your shovel and smack the largest, nastiest one in the muzzle with your tool. He is momentarily stunned, but soon he anchors himself for another attack. Although your attention is focused on your demon, you notice that the others are busy with their own wolves. The bodies of wolves and monks litter the ground. When he attacks again you will meet him with the sharp end of your shovel, delving his throat like the hard winter soil.

Level 2 begins in the zendo, a converted barn. Like the monks, you are sitting on a cushion counting your breaths, which rise ghostly into chill air. One of the monks strikes a large metal gong and you all stand. The teacher enters. You perform 108 prostrations, pressing your forehead to the cool polished wood of the floor. You think you might pass out. You chant for half an hour, and then sit again on your cushion. After a few minutes the door opens a crack and a chicken walks in, past the huge mahogany statue of Guan Yin. It opens again and another chicken enters. Soon there are dozens of chickens in the zendo with you, each armed with razor blades on its claws, and you and the other Zen practitioners are fighting for your lives. You raise your zafu but your chicken, a large red rooster, slashes it to shreds. Tatters of black fabric and shreds of kapok fly past your ears. The air is a blizzard of feathers.

Level 5 begins outside the dokusan room. You are ready for your first interview with the teacher. You enter the room, bow to the teacher, and kneel in front of him. He offers you a cup of strong, hot tea, and asks if you have any questions for him. You say, my mother is dying, drop your cup and leap at him. You want to tear out his throat and taste his blood. He smells like tea and the hard clay soil of the garden. He is tough, and not very tasty, but no match for your strength and guile. Soon he is lying in a pool of blood on his cushion, and you run from the room and into the woods, howling like the animal you are.

Level 12 begins with you and the pack of demons watching from the woods as monks work in the garden. There is a new teacher telling the others what to do. The pack rushes from the woods, and you head straight for the teacher. You can already smell his blood. Suddenly the ground gives way and you plummet like a fallen angel into a freshly dug pit. You imagine the spikes planted at the bottom of the pit. But there is only emptiness to greet you. Meanwhile the monks make short work of the pack. They're getting better at dealing with demons. They watch you from the edge of the pit and throw you table scraps and rice soaked in tea. It's raining. You are cold and miserable as a dog. You lap the water which gathers at the bottom of the pit. It tastes like coal

Level 257—At the beginning of Level 257 you are human again. The monks will not let you into the zendo. You sleep in the outhouse and work in the garden. Your job today is to pick raspberries for the monks' breakfast. You walk the narrow rows picking berries. Bees fly past you. You know you will spend your next life as a slug if you eat a berry, but they are so juicy and ripe and their purple juice stains your fingers. Your bowl fills with berries, and soon there are bees gathering to the bowl. You've always been afraid of bees, ever since a bee stung you as a child. You spent a week in the hospital, a human turnip. Suddenly you realize that these are not ordinary bees, just as a swarm of them masses above you. You stand your ground and let these killer bees, the dark cloud of memory, pass through you as if you were an open door.

Level 499—You're back in the zendo! Never did incense smell so sweet, nor 108 prostrations feel so exhilarating. The gong rings, and you rise as the teacher enters. While you're chanting the Heart Sutra, the earth begins to rumble. A giant earthquake shakes the zendo. The statue of Guan Yin begins to teeter, and finally topples, crushing the teacher and two of the monks. The shaking continues, even more violently. Roof beams and rafters fall all about you. When the dust settles, only you and a few others survive. The teacher and most of the monks have been completely buried. You rise from your zafu and begin picking up the pieces. Your job is to rebuild the zendo. Now you are the teacher.

"I Hate This Tree"

"Márgarét, áre you gríeving
Over Goldengrove unleaving? . . .
It is the blight man was born for,
It is Margaret you mourn for."

—Gerard Manley Hopkins

Portrait of the Artist As a Young Fashionista

Here I am, three-years-old, already too big
for the stroller—some iconic beach, not
Malibu, it must be Venice, my Baby Docs

in the foreground—cuffed
coveralls (faded, stone-washed), black
turtleneck with pink polka dots,

my blonde Afro kinking
beneath the hood, pretty pink-lipped
smile—but that's not what you notice—

what you notice are the glasses—
like mom's, bright red, wing-tipped,
fully mirrored and adorably bug-eyed—

a hundred and twenty degrees
of palm trees and back lit frenzy—
tourists slumming and slum dwellers

rubbing shoulders on Speedway,
a naked man, two half-naked girls,
more Afros and a couple of big drums—

mom's off to the side, pointing me
in the direction of the crowd,
I remember sitting there—

we did it often enough—
that woman who could lose herself
so easily in looking—but what about

me, the child? What lay hidden
beneath those twin reflecting pools
so like the pleistocene watering holes

that lured giant sloth and mammoth,
sabre tooth and dire wolf to a sticky end,
forty thousand years of megafauna

stacked haphazard in a petroleum pipe?
Who did she become, that darkness,
engulfed by so much light?

Hymn to Ninkasi*

I'm two years old, crawling
determinedly along the gleaming
mahogany of my god-mother's

bar, every foot or two another pool
of refreshment, golden hued, snow-
capped, a ring of chill condensation

welling at its base. Oh goddess,
it was then I learned your goodness,
granter of effervescent cheer,

and I, who never knew my mother's nipple,
now the beneficiary of every tippler's
largesse. How they marveled, this toddler,

hoisting goddess-shaped glasses
to his unquenchable lips. You grant us
surcease of all human hardships,

pain and boredom and two-out line-drive
singles bringing the opponent's tying
and winning runs to the plate.

Oh golden one, shock and awn,
we run to you when nothing else will do
but the flowing water, the hulled grains,

the toasted wheat and barley, the malt
and aromatic herbs, which cleanse us
of care, even at the age of two

as we bow to you, stretching our short
selves like your Tigris, your
Euphrates, in full snoring prostration.

---

* Ninkasi is known as the Sumerian goddess of beer. 3800 years ago some early Charles Bukowski indited a Hymn to Ninkasi, which was basically a recipe for beer.

Horizon and Walls

That was the year I learned to fear airplanes,
their hawk's cry, talons lowered for the descent.

Father wore the kind of suit undertakers wear
on a first date. Every day he would disappear

like a migratory bird, and reappear later
like a spring storm. I remember sitting

at the dinner table in my own chair,
a tiny boat in a choppy sea,

while my sister, a small precise storm,
a waterspout, roiled the harbor of mother's lap.

Young as I was, I had grown too large
for a berth in that marina. Some wind was pushing

me out to sea and no amount of tacking
could take me back to where I began. I could see

my future out the living room window,
its mix of horizon and walls. I held my father's

razor in one hand, my penis in the other.
He was always staring in the bathroom

mirror, daubing the blood.
I was always changing my mind.

I loved touching mother's breasts,
the way a potter loves clay.

I was her clay, the vase in which she arranged
her loneliness. She had me when most women

are sliding into drydock. We were feathers
in his trophy case. At nap time I slept with the baby.

Her scalp smelled like a cup of milk. I held her
closer, breathing in the meadow

where the milk grew, listening to rain
rising quietly into the clouds.

The Case of the Missing Chicken Pot Pie

Every evening home from the office, my father,
Managing Director for Finance and Internal Audit,
inspected the contents of his pantry and fridge.
We couldn't eat dinner until he had balanced
food on hand plus mother's daily list of food
purchased and consumed with the previous day's
inventory. If things didn't add up, we'd all sit
at the table and listen while father explained
that snacking was stealing from ourselves.
Later, after we'd all gone to bed, he'd plan
our meals for the next day, with an eye to cost,
of course, but also on calories and overall
nutritional value. One evening, my father,
the Controller and Chief Legal Counsel,
discovered a missing chicken pot pie.
The fact that it was his favorite meal,
and that it was the last one, had nothing
to do, he said, with his decision to punish
us all, the one who'd eaten the pot pie,
the ones who refused to squeal on the culprit,
and mother, who should have been more vigilant
in her role as Inventory Control Clerk. So we sat
at the kitchen table until bedtime, staring at one another,
the pale grim faces of my brother and sisters,
my mother as she chewed her lip, my father
smiling as if he'd played the greatest joke
of his life. I wondered who would break.
I was sure little Margie or the baby
would rat me out, although it was all of us
buried that awful thing in the yard,
as if it were a dead squirrel or possum
we'd found in the the alley back of the house.
It was my idea, of course, the little cardboard
headstone engraved with the motto:
RIP MD/FIA C&CLC BA MA MBA

Sacrifice Fly

Like sleepers roused too early,
bugs stumble into the new grass
flexing their unpracticed limbs and wings,

each year earlier than the last.
And yet, they are as beautiful as ever,
glossy, iridescent, or matte black—

like everything new, they snatch
our attention. This little guy, buzzing
on the sill, desperately trying any way

out, just a minute ago was desperate
to find a way in. Is it instinct, judgment
or cunning that rouses this demented

earnestness? In a day or two,
he'll be nothing but husk,
brushed away by the softest

touch. As a child I feared
every insect—caterpillars,
beetles, bees, wasps, even mosquitoes

and ants. I'd wait in the Amazonia
of right field for some looping
ball, magically accelerated

into that little used corner
of the outfield, to bend my way,
scratching my ankles and instep

the whole time, enough sulfur—
my mother's gift—in my socks
to cover my legs to the knees.

I took my exile with good humor,
cheering my more athletic teammates
and steadfastly belitting our opponents—

nobatternobatternobatter,
cricketed the chatterbox in right.
And yet, I felt lonely out there,

just me, the chiggers and fireflies,
the suffocating humidity
and the moon arching overhead,

patiently nearing its apogee,
taunting me to measure
my patience with its own.

Rats and Squirrels

Last night gale-force winds buffeted the house.
Squirrels clung to palm trees like shingles to the roof
and rats cowered in their nests while the wind

ruffled their fur like a mother stroking
her baby's blanket. Only the wind cares for rats.
A squirrel might be nutty, but there's something cheesy

about rats. Even if her feather boa is ratty,
a squirrel's tail is fluffy, whereas a rat's tail
is always naked as a stiletto. Who suffers

their hair to the misery of a rat-tail comb
or their wrought iron to a rat-tail file
but the poor in spirit and bank book?

Who doesn't prefer the hopping vegan,
always threatened, ever vulnerable,
to the slinking nocturnal scavenger,

bubonic pet, rodent of the apocalypse?
Which is less forbidding, the animal
world's Uriah Heep, squirreling

away her hoard against winter's cruelty,
or the Scrooge-like pack rat, miserly
to no good or end, a thief at the mercy

of his own compulsion? Does your boyfriend
belong to a rat pack? So much the worse for you.
When he couldn't keep a job or his driving license,

and his buck teeth seemed to glow in the dark,
he was just squirrelly. But now that he's stealing
your cash, and spending it on another girl,

you know what he is. You don't need to say it.

Young Americans for Freedom

There we were, four or five seminarians, in the back
of the auditorium, almost spilling over the lip
of the mezzanine, waiting for the man of the moment

to appear. He was a Jew, and we his sworn enemies—
politics makes strange bedfellows, that's what I was
told—and before we'd lose our country to godless

Communists, we'd makes allies of the Devil
and his spawn. That sounded okay to me, although
I'd never met an atheist, much less a Communist.

The Devil, however, was familiar, a constant companion,
always urging me to take another path, constantly
pointing out how narrow the high wire I trod, how deep

the drop. I stared at the crowd, the hats, hairnets and bald spots
below me. The music crescendoed and there he was,
the Senator from Arizona, polished, patrician, silver-

haired, tribune of the gainfully retired, refugees
from the Snow Belt, its frostbite and cinders.
We are surrounded by enemies, he told us,

not just in Asia and Europe, but in our own country,
people who would take our homes and businesses,
take away our beliefs, troublemakers

who want to sit next to you at lunch counters,
who'd force you to accept them as equals.
Freedom is a gift we have to protect from those

jealous of our freedoms. I'd learned enough
about the Virtue of Selfishness to know that taxes
are bad, that government saps your moral strength,

Delilah clipping Samson's hair. We'd been taught to look
in the mirror and see Satan. We had so many names for evil:
beatniks and the UN, homosexuals, secularism,

civil rights, the Federal Reserve—so many lions,
so few Daniels. Water cannons and police dogs
weren't enough, not riot police nor even Bull Connor

spitting into a bull horn—when would we realize
that all our weapons would never save us,
not until we declared war on America?

Magnolia

> O . . . *great-rooted blossomer*
> *are you the leaf, the blossom or the bole?*
>   — W.B. Yeats

"I hate this tree"—the first words from my new neighbor
bending over the ground cover beneath her magnolia,

Belle of the Old South, "sweet and fresh,"
subtropical exile to our fertile desert.

She was 80 or 85, the tree half her age
and tall as a three-story house,

still dropping leaves and seed pods
like a teenager with a bad case of dandruff.

"It killed my lawn," she said,
a violation twenty years in the past, which she held onto

as if it were last year, or last week. It soothed
and fueled her anger, I imagined, to pluck the brown

papery leaves from their hiding place in ivy
and stuff them in a green bin. I wondered if Sisyphus

hated his rock as much as she hated that tree.
I knew how much I hated my job, eight or nine

hours every day trying to lift the world another inch.
And every night more leaves would fall, leaves

and pods, those sexual hand grenades, those
pregnant cluster bombs. And yet she could no more live

without the tree than she could without her anger.
They were like an old couple, so deformed

by their love that they couldn't want anything else.
Every day after work I'd come home and find her,

bowed or kneeling, or toward the end just sitting in the ivy—
city of beetles, city of mice—and see the tree,

its orange and ruby lights blazoned with sunset's gilt.

Top of the Chain

Sometimes I see the stock boy from Lucky's
walking along the street. He's friendly
in the store, polite, suspicious,

but here he doesn't recognize me,
or any of the other passers-by,
most of whom must be Lucky's customers—

it's the only game in town.
But there he goes, in his white shirt and black
trousers, his Lucky's apron already

cinched to his chubby body.
He's got the gift of not looking anyone
in the eye, a lifetime's practice perhaps

perfecting shyness, and low self-esteem.
The checkers with their purple and green
streaks are brassier and ask how your day

is going. "Fine," I'll say, "and yours?"
"Okay," they'll say, after a quick double-take.
They know their job, even if they don't

know the code for fennel, which is marked
as sweet anise on their list of codes.
Get the shoppers out the door

so you can take your break,
a quick fifteen minutes with cigarette
and cell phone crouching on the curb

furthest from the door. The shrunken woman
who bags your groceries has some disease—
her eyes are sunken and always black—

or else she's got a husband on disability
who beats her when she gets home.
The guy who checks prices, his head is lopsided,

his glasses never straight on his face.
The butchers are helpful.
They've got a union and make real money,

although the one who weighed my sand dabs
has the cheeks and burst capillaries
of a devout alcoholic. I don't know

about you, but I'm always anxious to leave, another
failed reunion with relatives I didn't know I had.

For I Will Consider My Dog Riley

For that he vocalizes in different keys
          and registers, an opera singer with bite

For that he springs like a cricket
          when anyone approaches the door

For that he spins likes a dervish
          whene'er the word "food" is spoken

For that once he ran out any door or gate
          toward his erstwhile home, but no more

For that he overturns garbage pails
          and eats voluminously thereof

For that he eats other dogs' turds

For that he permits my daughter
          to scoop him into her arms

and lets her press him to her
          burgeoning breasts

For that he licks her tirelessly
          on the lips while she coos to him

For that he snaps at two-year-olds,
          causing them to cry

For that he barks at every garbage man
          and gardener who comes within hearing

the roar of the leaf blower
          a cause for raucous duets

For that he bites your oldest friend
          the moment he crosses the threshold

drawing blood from three lascivious
        punctures

For that he sits on your lap and breathes
        his doggy breath directly into your mouth

For that he is a moral philosopher
        measuring the needs of others against his own

and judging them inadequately voracious

for that he barks in warning but never in fear,
        in anger but never in despair

For that upon receiving a bath he immediately
        rolls in dirt

thereby drying himself and
        refreshing his doggy odor

For these and other reasons
        I adjudge him most exemplary of pets

derelict companion, loyal interrogator
        shadow and mimic, fiend and friend.

Butterfly

It's the damndest thing, seeing some big-name Hollywood actress
on the screen getting ready to jump off a building or a cliff
and knowing that's my girl, actually doing the crazy stuff.

When it comes to bodies flying through the air, she's the one
they go to first. She's been that way ever since she was little,
scaling her mom's etagére like it was some climbing wall.

You never heard such racket, her mom screaming about all her
precious knickknacks, and the little girl laughing like it was
Saturday morning cartoons. There was always casualties.

Usually the little girl's butt. But that didn't stop her. I'd come home
from work and the old lady'd be in the kitchen telling me to go look
for her, she'd lost the kid. How do you lose a three-year-old?

I'll tell you. I'd start in the back yard. We had us a couple of apple
trees, good size, and a magnolia, but I guess that was too simple,
like them jungle gyms at the playground. She was never interested in
> those.

Then I'd try the attic, but that was just for hiding, not climbing
and hiding, which was her speciality. And sure enough, there she'd be,
top of some closet, in among the hats or flashlights, who knows how
> long.

She never came out on her own, always needed someone to find her.
Already working on her legend. Back then she was just a kid,
but everybody in the neighborhood said she was something

else. Long before the barrel racing and dirt bike jumping.
I remember one time she was six or seven, and one of the neighbors
was having a backyard birthday party for one of theirs.

A couple of tables, a bunch of chairs, a barbecue pit
in no particular order, all over the lawn. And suddenly
there she was standing on top of one of them tables, and somebody's
    dad

(maybe it was me, I was pretty drunk) is yelling at her to get her
butt off the table, and she says, "Make me." Just like that, "Make me."
Defiant as a cockroach at three a.m.

So whoever the damn fool was lunges for her. Misses her, of course,
cuz she was off to the next table, only instead of taking the direct
route, across the lawn, she hops from chair to chair before

coming in for a landing, one foot in the sheet cake.
(Too bad about that cake. It had a nice portrait of the birthday girl.)
So the damn fool lunged again, missed again, landed in what

was left of the cake, because she's off, leaping from chair to table
to barbecue, like it was the most natural thing, and of course all those
things was getting upset and knocked over, but she just kept going

round and around the yard (never once setting foot on the ground),
whatever she landed on, upright or upside down, she was on to the
    next thing,
like she was a butterfly trying out all the flowers in the garden.

That's when I knew I weren't never gonna be the regular kind of dad,
no sir. I was going be the dad you read about in them movie star
    biographies,
the guy who after you're done with the book gets to pick up the pieces.

Clipped

Maybe I've stopped
thinking I want
anything out
of this life not
even a poet's small
oxymoronic
fame this morning
I took my daughter
through streets tender
with petals, spring
& all, for a haircut
even though it wasn't
long just thicker like a
blackberry bush
in the middle
of summer you can't
see into or even
through the dark curls
snatching light
like one of those
black holes
astronomers
tell us live in
the center of
galaxies that will
swallow everything
atoms & all
by the end of time
what we can't see
pulls on us trapping
even our light
although it's all
just a story
unless you believe
in mathematics

and the incorporeal
steel of Occam's
razor thinking that
yes, I believe,
even as a woman
scooped the billows
snipping auburn
fractals soft
at her feet me
thinking maybe only
the thinking has
stopped, but not
the wanting

Culture Vultures

. . . only the fact of her husband
. . . kept me from springing on her
or falling at her little feet and crying
'You are the hottest one for years of night
Henry's dazed eyes
have enjoyed, Brilliance.'

—John Berryman

Wirtschaftswunderkind

the Divided City

School was an insult, every day taking orders
from some former Group Leader or Hauptmann,
all of them hastily retired from the Nazi Party

and the Waffen-SS, pretending everything
now was normal, the new apocalypse waiting just
over the horizon. Many days I'd board

the S-Bahn and circle the city,
passing school a dozen times, passing through
British, French, American, and finally

the Russian Zone of Occupation—
forests, lakes, and houses, the half million animals
locked in the zoo, the elephant's

long brown penis as defiant as its tusks.
I loved my city: the ladies with their bloated ankles
and bleeding gums, the Bürgers in their tiny

Alpine caps, each trimmed with an identical
pheasant feather, university girls careless
of their appearance, shopgirls

skilled at anorexia.
How many times did the Rector threaten
to throw me out, the school's best student,

scion of his wife's favorite doctor?
What kind of boy skips school, my parents
wanted to know? I was a good student,

my teachers told them—someday I too
might become a teacher. I was studying, I told them,
which was true, working the most difficult

chess problems I could find. By my last year, I was
making them up myself. By my last year
I was champion of the whole city,

all four parts, one better than Caesar.
Maybe I had too many distractions.
I loved smashing volleyballs

into an opponent's face, tramping
through mud along hedges and ditches,
the one thing I wouldn't do—a soldier.

Bundeswehr, Wehrmacht—who could tell the difference?
Later, I drove my tiny Porsche fast as a Formula 1
racer, from the encircled city to Ostend

in less than 2 hours. People say I like to argue
and that when I drink too much, I throw up.
That's true, but only to make a point.

Many Are Called

Arbeit macht frei*

You want to pen the definitive study,
the last word. And so you pore through
each new issue of the Humanities
Index for any articles about your man.

Almost every day another article arrives
in the post. Each one requires careful reading,
the taking of notes, the judging of its worth,
an estimate of its impact on your overall

thesis. You've been at it 10 years.
Meanwhile your wife is waiting
for that first professorship,
the opportunity to have a child.

Why, she thinks, was teaching
in the Gymnasium not good enough?
In the mean time, you run errands for your
professor, your 'Doctor Father,' showing

a "guest" professor around town, taking him
to register with the police, finding
him a room. He's not a bad guy,
the visitor, just helpless. You

feel sorry for him, never been
out of his own country before.
He reminds you of yourself,
a high school student in the same

backward town he came from.
He's funny, uses language
like a spray bottle, misting
your soul with wit. He calls himself

---

* The phrase meaning "work makes one free" appeared over the entrance to Auschwitz and other Nazi concentration camps.

a "culture vulture," the sound of which
pleases your wife. All three of you
have had too much to drink,
the good stuff from home, your little river

valley, sweeter than the French,
but tangy with limestone and clay.
Do you really need to read everything,
he asks, the same question your wife

asks at least once a year?
Arbeit macht Spaß, your guest exclaims,
a parrot cracking walnuts with
its beak. What's stopping you

from starting—the question
in everyone's mind, but especially
yours? It's raining outside.
It's always raining outside. Time

for your guest to leave. You could
drive him into town, but another
packet of articles arrived today,
and you need to get back to work.

Match

> *So it's war again, Venus, after all this time.*
> —Horace

She's a bitch, always throwing you out
just when you start to have fun.
Lets her hair down, then complains
when you catch your fingers in the coils.
Opens the top two buttons of her blouse,
then faults you for staring into the abyss.
"It's hot," she'll say, "but you're too hot."

Let her toy with some over-eager boy
half my age, who's never sat across from her
transfixed by the play of candlelight in her eyes.
Let her grant his dearest wish,
set tinder to the kindling of his desire
and watch the whole man burn, heretic and martyr,
heaping the fuel of hopefulness on his own pyre.

Are any still left in this cynical age,
who follow the goddess and throw their riches—
curly hair, abs like a drum head—at her feet?
What do they know, who ignore her power,
she who lights the darkest sky with wind shear
and the temperature gradient of lust?
She can drive straw like nails through wrists and feet.

But let me be. I've done my time,
as my friends are tired of hearing.
I've worn myself out chasing Lydia and Cynara
from one decade to the next. Even they,
who used to light my auto-da-fé, leave me cold.
Wine too, and all the other hungers
that seemed more real than myself.

Why is it then, Ava-Noel, I stop
sometimes mid-sentence to stare at mountains
as they chart the horizon's irregular heartbeat?
And why in dreams do I find myself
chasing you across six lanes
of freeway traffic just as earth
loosens her girdle and begins to shake?

No Sweat (the Step Reebok Poem)

Those were the years I was up by six
and in the gym half an hour later,
disco booming in my ears.

I was better than half way through
my forties, but still climbing my own
personal Dhaulagiri. Don't ask me

about my job or about the girl
I was living with. So much was missing
from my life that I needed to exhaust

the complainer before he could get started.
Me in my sleeveless tee, my bike shorts
and sweat band—me and the girls—

almost a dance (this was before zumba
or jazzercize), stepping on and over
a pile of plastic trays, gently as if it were the grave

of memory, walking around it, the hole
in the center of my life, pumping
a leg, one, two or three times,

trying to shake off whatever still
clung to me of childhood and parents,
repeating the movements on the other

side, always the other side, trying
to maintain balance, lest I topple
from that summit and tumble

into some abyss I'd been digging
my whole life. You see
the futility of it all. And yet I

savored my futility, it was something
only I could do, poised there and
gathering myself for the next step.

Kaffee mit Schlag

before it arrives on the dock at Le Havre, Ostend or Bremen, it ripens on tiny trees in the cloud forest

six thousand feet above sea level, strato cumulus, patient gardeners, bringing a hundred inches every year

the temperature never below seventy

you remember we walked there, a canopied walkway, the winter after your surgery, the first surgery

we talked about the violence in our own country, the police unable to stop themselves from killing innocents

and the violence in that country, the peasants who tended the trees taking machetes to their light-skinned managers, invasive growth

you quipped, the surgeon had done as much for you, leaving a clearing where once lung had been

you wondered where the next red x might appear—kidney, pancreas, the other lung

the body is its own kind of geography

we learned that earlier, with other lovers, mapping our thrills, exploring our discontent like rock climbers more than half in love with easeful death

those quotes, that freeze-dried learning, how we enjoyed it, tramping the tourist trails, protected from everything but the future

here, at the biggest little Konditorei in Vienna, I've set a place for you, your own cup and pot of bitter brew, as if you were the Sybil about to report on the future a future different from the one I see, the tunnel at the end of the light

can you smell it, the seeds rushed from some North Sea harbor in refrigerated trucks and roasted to a soft auburn glow, seeds that want only to grow other seeds, trees and seeds, but whose toxins stimulate our interest in ourselves and the lives around us, simulate a fuller kind of life, ground into powder, steamed in a mechanical volcano

a plate of baked delicacies between us, although there is nothing between us now

(how you loved their napoleons, I the Schwarzwalderkirschtorte)

Aeneas did as much for his lost companions

which is not to say I'm in hell, not at all, but someplace much worse

the designated mourner who can't stop loving this life

Peeling the Onion

Not the tough papery skin
nor the translucent layer just beneath

but the onion part of the onion,
the part that makes you cry,

the solid muscle of the onion,
its bitter white heart.

Cook it long enough it sweetens,
grows tender, shrinking into

some truer self, the self
it becomes as it ferments in the body.

Imagine standing all day in a kitchen
your only job slicing onions—

slicing and breading the slices
and sliding them into a bubbling vat.

What would you have learned
after a day, after a month—

after a lifetime of slicing,
examining each layer and slice

for whatever makes the onion unique,
the essential onion,

its perfected self? It is onion
all the way in, reservoir and fibre,

a gift. Now look at yourself.
You are nothing like an onion.

Whatever hides beneath
the skin is irrelevant.

You are a seed, surrounded by
fruit, your only hope

to plant yourself in fertile soil.
What will become of you

who have known only the one tree,
the one soil? Where will you land

once water and wind have their way with you?
How long will you struggle

to find some parable of growth?
Consider the onion resting for the moment

on your chopping board,
a victim of the Terror, the head of some

mythical beast—your head,
inert, and peaceful at last.

Belles de Jour

> *Mais où sont les neiges d'antan!*

How could I not love you?
You were the sister I never had,
compensation for two dead brothers.

You remember that cafe in the Fourth?
You pointing at the galaxy circling
in your latté, as if to remind me of the night

twenty years before—we were standing in the rain
in front of the Los Feliz arguing
about Godard, whether he was God

or Godot. I still remember the movie,
2 or 3 Things I Know about Her, Her
being Paris, Her being you.

Was that why we started going there
every year? At first it was all about the guys,
the Frenchmen, the Algerians, the black

Africans, all that latent fire.
We traded them back and forth,
rating them like movies while we watched

the mise-en-scène along the Boule Miche,
sipping double and triple shots,
trying to get sober.

I never felt married when I was with you,
even though most of the time some man
in LA was spending my money

and watching my son. Roma
and Jew, our two peoples migratory
as storks, Kentucky and the Bronx,

always living near a border
in case some night we needed to
slip across. What was his name,

that half-black kid you called Le Petit Prince
of the banlieues? He was tender enough in bed,
but fierce too. How much did he blame us

for the roaches and the shitty schools,
the hate in every white Frenchman's eyes?
We were amusantes, and greedy,

and he didn't care if we were older—
we spent our money on him,
the first pair of sneakers that hadn't

belonged to one of his brothers.
He was our Belmondo.
You told me he was shot

holding a lighted Molotov. And then I saw you
two together near Montparnasse.
That was mean. But live long enough,

you get over everything. Besides,
I took one or two away from you.
And now we're back in Paris,

trying even harder to look younger.
Here's to Catherine Deneuve!
What you lose in body you gain in character.

There are more of him than ever on the streets,
more hate. Let's sip our aperitifs and watch others
make all the mistakes we worked so hard to make.

Boardom

> "Sunbathers in a busy Berlin park were treated to the sight of a naked man chasing after a wild boar which was carrying his belongings."
> — The Independent

they're not there then suddenly
you see them dash from the brush
a sow and two piglets

heading for the bag where you've stowed
your clothes and lunch—
some bread, a wedge of cheese, a pear—

these relics of an earlier time
when forests ruled the land
and wolves ruled the forest

here at Teufelssee (Devil's Lake)
surrounded by what remains
of the forest's rank and musky self

its permanent dusk
its spine and crumbling splendor
arms uplifted in permanent prayer

how long has this taming taken—
you walk into a toy store
and there she is, soft and tiny

(in the wild taller than a child)
our nephews and nieces in bed
cuddling the plush synthetics

her tiny plastic tusks a threat
only in the imagination—the girl
in the red cape would know

to listen for a sudden rustle in the bushes
(what we dreamed, some rough beast in rut)
and hurry in another direction, all of them away

and yet here we loll in the altogether
on the shore of the Apocalypse
at a beach called Instant Gratification

watching the spectacle (a spectacle ourselves,
not even a pink triangle for cover)
a naked man chasing animals naked too

except for a bright orange bag,
gentle reminder of how long
it took to achieve this indolence

how quickly it might disappear

Forgetfulness

after Billy Collins

The name of the person is first to go,
and then the color of her eyes, the crinkle
at the corner of her lips, her heart-melting sigh.
Was she real or just a frolicsome phantom,

and what of that city where you might have met,
its stagnant lagoon, the rush of storm water,
the way the rain fashioned a snood from her hair
and brightened her cheeks, her lips, her hooded eyes?

You were her confessor, or was that someone else?
You listened, you're almost sure, to her tale—
in some charmingly accented version of your language—
or was it hers?—of her flight from oppression—

her boyfriend, or husband, some privateer of the heart,
who boarded, then abandoned her, to float
becalmed in the horse latitudes of despair,
returning occasionally to rummage for some small

overlooked treasure. You've told the tale yourself,
dozens, if not hundreds of times—each time
losing some memento, paltry, unimportant—
that imposing derelict rising smartly from the windswept

beach of your memory, wrapped now
in fog that thickens with age.

Not Brave, Not Free

after Tony Hoagland

All morning some virus has been conducting
military exercises in my throat—
napalm, aerial bombardment, artillery.

Bombing the dam was the last straw.
"You sound sick," my wife says
solicitously. "No I don't," I insist,

struck by the uncharacteristic rumble
of my vocal chords, the basso profundo
echoing in my ear bones. "I sound sexy."

I wonder if my penchant for lying
to myself is a personal peccadillo,
or something hard-wired into all of us.

I know that, I know that, says the kid
in the back row, face red as a stop sign,
hand waving, high in the air.

I ignore him. After all, I'm the teacher
in this little classroom, and even though I too
know the answer, I need to pretend I don't.

Like those balloon faces floating on my TV,
asking if, after the latest shooting, the President
will finally bring the nation together.

They know the answer, but their investment
in our collective stupidity is building interest
in Switzerland and the Cayman Islands.

Meanwhile California redwoods,
the few survivors, are in emergency conclave.
"Where's the fog?" they want to know. I know,

but have no way of telling them.

Passing an Evening, Not Quite Drunk

I confess. I can barely stand
myself. Can you imagine? Perhaps
you've never experienced vertigo like this,
this Jimmy Stewart moment
seated at a long table beneath a large tree

surrounded by uncomprehending friends.
What was it I said—nothing personal
or abusive—something allusive, as is my habit,
and mock rhetorical, everything in quotes,
as if I were quoting something quite unbelievable

even though the words were my own.
Perhaps the squadrons of flying insects,
almost invisible, which rose at dusk,
disconcerted everyone and everything, the food,
the drink, the gentle accommodating conversation.

It might have been the whine, so like a distant jet
targeting our innocent gathering, that set people on edge.
But I was sure it was me, so characteristically indirect
and cautious. "Those children," I exclaimed, "those poor
children snatched from the mothers,

handed over to strangers, well-meaning no doubt,
whose most fervent prayer is to win them
from the life their parents might have given them,
a life of poverty and struggle. Surely they would benefit
in obvious ways, raised and surrounded by people like us,

but wouldn't they always be strangers to us,
just as we'd be strangers to them?"
And as if I had not said enough already,
I quoted the one person I never quote.
"Jesus said to welcome the stranger, I think,

not kidnap them." Despite the setting
this was no Swedish comedy, nor even its re-make
by Woody Allen. No one was interested in any of the bodies
seated at the table, except possibly their own.
What might have ended in a comfortably dissipated fog,

this evening of friendship, of laugher and agreeable mocking,
had suffered abrupt rupture, and I, unwitting terrorist,
armed only with the explosives in my head, had destroyed it,
this unrecoverable moment. Or so I thought. Things seemed
very different then, the conversation dying,

the drone of engines closer, people swatting invisible
attackers with spasmodic fervor, slapping arms and cheeks.
I'm drunk, ignore me, I should have said, but despite the knowledge
that I'd be judged and found guilty, issued no disclaimer.
I left then, aware that my mistake had been deliberate—

one of those choices one makes without premeditation
or even awareness, it is so much a part of one's nature,
a despised and neglected part perhaps,
but no less true for being shunned—
knowing now I might never return.

Journée Internationale de la Bisexualité

It's our 20th wedding anniversary
but also International Bisexuality Day.

What a lovely coincidence!
People flagrantly smooching

on the streets of Paris and the two of us
walking hand in hand past gay Parisian

shops, one that calls itself "i do MARIAGE"
and another named 'small,' a smartcar

parked in front. We spend all day
examining the latest bras and heels,

the newest tourists and tourist traps.
And what about the Lego hooker

(in primary colors) pasted high on a wall,
her pixellated contours

the latest in pubic art?
Hemingway called Paris a Moveable Feast,

but feast feels too sedate
for this orgy, this bachanal of looking

and loving. Young couples (Gallic as Asterix)
push perambulators past the Pompidou

and play with their toddlers on the grimy flagstones,
beneficiaries of the government's largesse

and fear of Algerians—who also happen to be
French citizens—juicing procreation

as if it were jihad. It's all a bit confusing
to those of us, visitors from Puritania,

for whom a plein air peck is an act of daring,
who save the French stuff for behind closed doors.

Ultimo

underwater

I forget to hold my breath
but do as I do on rooftops
or in the varied spaces
beneath trees and yet
I'm surprised when
I don't lose consciousness
its large clumsy weave
streamlined as fish
I should know that
something has changed
or I have changed
but am enough content
in this wide and luminous
place touched by light
on all sides to move
as one moves whose
only motive is joy

About the Author

Lee Rossi was born in St. Louis, Missouri, in another century. He studied five years for the Roman Catholic priesthood before leaving the seminary, and devoting himself to the study of failure. He draws inspiration from poets living and dead, and in the past twenty years has met as many fine and superfine not yet dead poets as he can. His ultimate concerns as a poet can best be gauged by an excerpt from a posthumous interview with the German poet Rainer Maria Rilke:

> Rossi: *Angels and art are all well and good, but what about an age like this one that only cares about self-aggrandizement?*
>
> Rilke: *Only after the Self has been abraded by Ridicule and Catastrophe can it approach the Truly Momentous.*

Rossi is the author of four books of poetry, *Darwin's Garden* (Moon Tide Press, 2019), *Wheelchair Samurai* (Plainview Press, 2011), *Ghost Diary* (Terrapin Press, 2003) and *Beyond Rescue* (Bombshelter Press, 1992), and has appeared in numerous anthologies, including *Don't Leave Hungry: 50 Years of Southern Poetry Review* (University of Arkansas Press, 2010), *Blue Arc West* (Tebot Bach, 2006), *Chance of a Ghost* (Helicon Nine Editions, 2005), *Mischief, Caprice, & Other Strategies* (Red Hen Press, 2002) and *Grand Passion: the Poetry of Los Angeles and Beyond* (Red Wind Books, 1995).

His poems have appeared in many journals, including *The Harvard Review, Poetry Northwest, The North American Review, Main Street Rag,*

Tar River Poetry, The Spoon River Poetry Review, The Southeast Review, The Atlanta Review, The Green Mountains Review, The Sun, Poetry East, Chelsea, The Wormwood Review, Nimrod, Beloit Poetry Journal, Poet Lore, The Southern Poetry Review, The Southern Indian Review, Poetry/LA, Onthebus and others. He has published reviews in *88: A Journal of Contemporary American Poetry, Poetry International, Smartish Pace, Poetry Flash, The Los Angeles Review,* and the online journal *Pedestal.* He is a winner of the Sense of Site poetry contest sponsored by the Los Angeles Cultural Affairs Department and The Jack Grapes Poetry Prize. From 1986 to 1992, he edited *Tsunami,* a journal of contemporary poetry focused on Los Angeles. He is a member of the Northern California Book Reviewers and a Contributing Editor for *Poetry Flash.*

Acknowledgments

Grateful acknowledgment is made to the editors of the following journals in which some of these poems have previously appeared:
Atlanta Review: "Match"
The Aurorean: "Forgetfulness"
Birdland Journal: "Magnolia"
Caesura: "Gone Wild" & "Spirit Train"
The Chiron Review: "Cricket"
Cultural Daily: "Not Brave, Not Free"
Dark Ink (a Horror Anthology): "Close Encounters of Another Kind"
Green Hills Literary Lantern: "The Retired Epistemologist" (appeared as "The Lazy Epistemologist") and "No! Not That!"
Humble Pie: "Journée Internationale de la Bisexualité"
I'll Be You When You Get There (an online anthology): "Instructions to My Teenage Self"
The I-70 Review: "Sacrifice Fly"
The Lindenwood Review: "Zen: the Video Game"
Paterson Literary Review: "The International House of Insomnia," "Consider This"
Poet Lore: "Rules of Thumb" and "Scenes from the Other Life"
Portside.org: "Young Americans for Freedom"
Plainsongs: "Sebastian to His Wounds"
Rattle: "microcosmology"
San Diego Poetry Annual: "Say Anything," "Portrait of the Artist as a Young Fashionista," "Butterfly"
The Southwest Review: "Clipped"
Spillway: "The Case of the Missing Chicken Pot Pie"
The Tinderbox Review: "The Angel Angle"

Thanks also to all the lovely and astute folks who have read earlier versions of this work: Charlotte Muse, Peter Carroll, Esther Kamkar, Terry Adams, Anne Cheliek, Mary Bailey, Brenda Simmons, Diane Schenker, & Steve Rood. Thanks also to Beth Nelson for her encouragement and for putting me in touch with the fabulous photographer, Loretta Young-Gautier.

www.ingramcontent.com/pod-product-compliance
Lightning Source LLC
Chambersburg PA
CBHW050040080526
44586CB00014B/1387